THE GOSPEL OF THE KINGDOM

Rediscovering the Full Message of Jesus

Salvation · Healing · Empowerment · The Hope of Christ's Return

Nick Booth

Contents

Foreword

There are moments in church history when the people of God are called back to something they have allowed to slip from their grasp — not because it was taken from them, but because, slowly and almost imperceptibly, they set it down.

The message you are about to read is one such reclamation. It is a call to pick up what has been set aside.

In many parts of the Western church, the Gospel has been quietly trimmed and tidied. We have kept the parts that are easiest to defend in polite conversation and softened the parts that sound too wild, too supernatural, or too urgent. We have kept a Saviour but lost the Healer. We have retained the Holy Spirit in our creeds but quenched Him in our meetings. We have nodded at Christ's return as a distant theological footnote while our neighbours live and die with no urgency, and no hope.

This book does not argue for novelty. It argues for recovery. Its thesis is as old as the New Testament itself: that the Gospel Jesus preached — and the Gospel that turned the ancient world upside down — was a fourfold declaration. Jesus saves. Jesus heals. Jesus baptises with the Holy Spirit. And Jesus is coming again.

These four truths are not the private property of any denomination. They were the common currency of the early church in the first century, and they became the defining marks of the great global awakening of the twentieth and twenty-first centuries. Where these four convictions are preached with faith and demonstrated with power, the church has never failed to grow. Where they are neglected, the church has tended to shrink — first in vitality, then in numbers.

The author writes not as a detached theologian but as a pastor, evangelist, and practitioner who has seen these truths confirmed in lived experience — in families restored, bodies healed, lives transformed by the Spirit's power, and hearts set ablaze by the expectation of Christ's return.

May the pages that follow stir in you a holy hunger. May you discover, or rediscover, just how big the Gospel truly is.

A Note on the Fourfold Gospel

The framing of Christ as Saviour, Healer, Baptiser in the Holy Spirit, and Coming King did not originate with this book. It has a history worth knowing.

In 1887, Albert Benjamin Simpson — founder of the Christian and Missionary Alliance — preached a series of sermons he called The Fourfold Gospel, presenting Christ as Saviour, Sanctifier, Healer, and Coming King. It was the first time these four convictions had been gathered into a single, cohesive theological framework, and it shaped the entire Holiness and early Pentecostal movements that followed. Simpson's contribution to evangelical missionary theology is immense, and this book owes him more than a footnote.

Thirty-five years later, Aimee Semple McPherson — founder of the International Church of the Foursquare Gospel — preached what she called the Foursquare Gospel, adapting Simpson's framework into its Pentecostal form: Christ as Saviour, Baptiser in the Holy Spirit, Healer, and Coming King. McPherson's version became the heartbeat of the charismatic renewal that has spread across the world in the century since. It is her formulation — Baptiser rather than Sanctifier — that most closely reflects the language used in this book.

So why not simply use the language of one of these movements? Because the Complete Gospel is not the property of any movement. It is the testimony of Scripture. Christ heals not because the Christian and Missionary Alliance says so, but because Isaiah 53 says so, because Acts 10:38 says so, because the Gospels record it on nearly every page. Christ baptises in the Holy Spirit not because the Foursquare Church holds it as a doctrinal position, but because John the Baptist announced it, because Jesus promised it, and because the church at Pentecost experienced it. The Coming King is not an end-times theological preference — it is the unanimous expectation of the New Testament.

The four convictions in this book are presented as biblical truth, not denominational distinctive. Readers from every tradition — Anglican, Baptist, Presbyterian, Pentecostal, charismatic, and independent — will find them here because they belong to all of us. They are not the innovation of any one teacher or movement. They are the full portrait of Jesus that the whole Bible paints.

To Simpson and McPherson, and to the countless preachers and missionaries who have carried this message to the ends of the earth: this work stands on your shoulders.

Introduction

How Big Is Your Gospel?

Let me ask you a question before we begin. Not a trick question — but an honest one, the kind worth sitting with for a moment.

How big is your Gospel?

For many Christians, the Gospel is primarily a transaction: I was a sinner, Jesus died for my sins, I prayed a prayer, and now I am going to heaven when I die. That is gloriously, wonderfully true. But is it the whole truth? Is that really the full scope of what Jesus came to accomplish — and what He commissioned His church to proclaim?

When we look at the two periods in church history that produced the most extraordinary expansion of Christianity — the first century church described in the opening chapters of Acts, and the global Pentecostal and Charismatic movement of the twentieth and twenty-first centuries — a striking pattern emerges. Both movements shared four convictions that were not incidental to their preaching but absolutely central to it:

Christ is Saviour — the only name by which human beings can be saved. Christ is Healer — the same compassionate Lord who healed the sick in Galilee heals today. Christ is the Baptiser — who immerses His followers in the Holy Spirit and empowers them for witness. Christ is coming again — and this urgency shapes everything about how we live and how we love.

These four convictions together are sometimes called the Foursquare Gospel — a phrase that originates with the revival movements of the early twentieth century but describes a pattern visible all the way back to the ministry of Jesus and the earliest apostolic preaching.

This book is an exploration of each of these four dimensions. It is written for followers of Jesus who want to understand the full scope of what they have received in Christ. It is written for churches that sense something is missing and are hungry to recover it. And it is written for anyone who has ever wondered whether there might be more to the Christian life than what they have so far experienced.

Dogma, Doctrine, and Teaching

Before we begin, a brief word about how we handle disagreement. Within Christianity there are matters of Dogma — non-negotiable truths without which we are no longer within orthodox Christian faith. The Trinity. The Virgin Birth. The physical resurrection of Jesus. All true Christians everywhere agree on these. Then there is Doctrine — important convictions on which sincere, Bible-believing Christians hold different views: the mode of baptism, the details of end-times chronology, questions of church governance. These differences should not divide us, even when we hold our views with conviction. Finally, there are Teachings — secondary matters about which we can discuss and even disagree without breaking the bond of Christian fellowship.

The chapters of this book range across all three of those categories. Some of what we discuss is Dogma. Some is Doctrine. Some is Teaching. I will try to be clear about which is which. Please receive it all with both an open Bible and an open hand.

How to Use This Book

Each chapter can be read on its own, but they are designed to be read in sequence — each dimension of the Gospel builds on and deepens the one before it. At the back of the book you will find a Study Guide designed for both individual reflection and group discussion. For each chapter it provides discussion questions, key scriptures to memorise, and personal reflection prompts to help move the content from your head into your life. If you are reading this as part of a small group or Bible study, the guide is written with you in mind. You may find it helpful to read each chapter before your group meets and bring your reflections ready to share.

Now — let us discover just how big this Gospel really is.

CHAPTER ONE

Christ Our Saviour

The Foundation of Everything

The Exclusive Claim

There is a verse in the book of Acts that has never lost its power to stop people in their tracks. The Apostle Peter, freshly filled with the Holy Spirit and standing before the religious authorities who had recently conspired to crucify his Lord, says something breathtaking in its simplicity and its audacity:

> *"Salvation is found in no one else, for there is no other name under heaven given to mankind by which we must be saved."* — **Acts 4:12**

No one else. No other name. In a world that was, even then, crowded with competing religious claims and rival philosophies, Peter draws a line in the dust. The salvation of human beings — real salvation, the kind that reaches the deepest need of the human soul — is available in one place and one place only: the person of Jesus of Nazareth.

This is a claim that makes many people deeply uncomfortable, and we should be honest about that. It sounds, to modern ears, intolerant. Exclusive. Even arrogant. But before we soften it or apologise for it, we need to sit with what it actually means — and why it is, at its heart, the most hopeful thing anyone has ever said.

The Problem That Demands a Solution

The starting point of the Gospel is an honest diagnosis of the human condition. The Bible has a word for what is wrong with us: sin. Not primarily the individual acts of wrongdoing, though those matter — but the fundamental orientation of the human heart away from God. The theological word for it is hamartia, which literally means 'missing the mark.' We were made for relationship with God, made to live within His design, and we have consistently — individually and collectively — chosen otherwise.

The consequences of this are not merely moral. They are existential. Sin creates a fracture between human beings and the God in whose image we are made. And because God is the source of life, separation from Him is, by definition, the beginning of death — not just physical death, but the spiritual death that Paul describes as being 'separated from the life of God' (Ephesians 4:18). No human effort can bridge this fracture. Not religious observance, not moral improvement, not philosophical wisdom, not the accumulation of good deeds.

The One Who Bridges the Gap

This is where the Gospel becomes the best news ever announced. Into the fracture that human beings cannot bridge, God Himself steps. The second person of the Trinity — the eternal Son of God — takes on human flesh and enters the world He made. He lives the life of perfect obedience that we were designed to live but have never managed. And then He takes upon Himself the consequence of our failure: death. The penalty for sin falls on Him rather than on us.

Paul puts it with breathtaking conciseness: 'God made him who had no sin to be sin for us, so that in him we might become the righteousness of God' (2 Corinthians 5:21). The sinless one becomes sin, so that the sinful ones might become righteous. It is the greatest exchange in history. And then, three days later, God raised Him from the dead. The resurrection is the Father's declaration that the sacrifice was accepted, the debt paid, the fracture healed. Death — the ultimate consequence of sin — has been defeated.

> *"I am the way and the truth and the life. No one comes to the Father except through me."* **— John 14:6**

He says it not to exclude people but to include them. Jesus is not guarding the door of heaven against gate-crashers. He is standing at the door, knocking, inviting anyone who will hear His voice to open it.

Receiving the Gift

Salvation, the New Testament tells us, is a gift. Not a reward. Not a wage. Not something we can claim as ours by right.

> *"For the wages of sin is death, but the gift of God is eternal life in Christ Jesus our Lord."* — **Romans 6:23**

How do we receive it? The New Testament gives us a clear and simple answer, sometimes summarised in three words: Accept, Believe, Confess. We accept what God has said about our condition and about His remedy. We believe in our hearts that Jesus is who He claimed to be: that He died for our sins, that God raised Him from the dead, and that He is Lord. And we confess — declare openly, with our mouths — that Jesus is Lord of our lives.

> *"If you declare with your mouth, 'Jesus is Lord,' and believe in your heart that God raised him from the dead, you will be saved."* — **Romans 10:9-10**

There is one more element that is essential to this transaction, and it is the word the Bible calls repentance. Repentance is not self-flagellation or an endless rehearsal of our failures. It means, quite simply, to turn around. To change direction. To say: I have been living as though God does not matter — and I recognise that this is wrong. I turn away from that old direction and I turn towards Jesus. This is not a grim or reluctant act. The Bible says that it is the goodness of God that leads us to repentance (Romans 2:4).

The Beginning, Not the End

Salvation is not the whole of the Gospel. It is the door through which we enter everything else. When we receive Christ, we are not simply given a ticket to heaven. We are born again by the Spirit of God — made genuinely new from the inside. We are adopted into the family of God, with all the rights and privileges of sonship. We are indwelt by the Holy Spirit, who begins the long and beautiful work of making us into the people we were always meant to be.

The Gospel of the Kingdom begins here. But as we will see in the chapters that follow, it does not end here.

CHAPTER TWO

Christ Our Healer

The God Who Touches

A Gospel That Touches Bodies

In the tenth chapter of Acts, the Apostle Peter stands in the home of a Roman centurion named Cornelius and delivers what may be the most compressed and powerful summary of the Gospel in the entire New Testament. He describes Jesus in a single, extraordinary sentence:

> *"God anointed Jesus of Nazareth with the Holy Spirit and with power, who went about doing good and healing all who were oppressed by the devil, for God was with him."* **— Acts 10:38**

Notice what Peter considers central to the story of Jesus: He went about doing good and healing all who were oppressed. Healing is not a footnote in the ministry of Jesus. It is not an embarrassing feature that the sophisticated modern believer needs to explain away. It is the natural outflow of who Jesus is — a God who is not content to save souls while leaving bodies broken.

The Gospel of the Kingdom has always been a holistic message. Jesus did not come to rescue an immaterial part of us called the soul while leaving the rest of our humanity untouched. He came to redeem the whole person — body, soul, and spirit. Healing is the evidence of that.

The Healing Ministry of Jesus

Open the Gospels anywhere and you will find Jesus healing people. A leper who had been excluded from society for years, finally able to come close to another human being. A paralysed man lowered through a roof by four determined friends. A woman who had spent twelve years and every penny she owned seeking a cure, healed in a moment by the touch of His garment. A blind man given sight. A deaf man given hearing. A dead girl restored to her family.

> *"When Jesus landed and saw a large crowd, he had compassion on them and healed their sick."* — **Matthew 14:14**

Compassion. The Greek word here — splagchnizomai — refers to a movement in the deepest part of a person's being. Jesus was moved in His gut by the sight of human suffering. Healing was not primarily a strategy for drawing crowds or demonstrating divine credentials, though it accomplished both. It was the natural expression of a God who loves people. And the New Testament is clear that this compassion did not die on the cross, nor was it buried in the tomb. The risen, ascended Christ remains the same in character as the Jesus who walked the roads of Galilee. The writer to the Hebrews tells us that He is the same yesterday, today, and forever (Hebrews 13:8).

The Question of Cessationism

At this point, some readers will raise an objection. They will have been taught — perhaps by sincere and well-meaning Bible teachers — that the age of miracles is over. That healing and the miraculous gifts of the Spirit were given to the church for a specific founding period, and that once the New Testament canon was complete, or once the last apostle died, God withdrew these gifts. This view is known as cessationism.

It is worth engaging with this view honestly, because it has shaped the expectations of many Christians and entire denominations. However, cessationism faces two significant problems.

First, it has no clear scriptural support. There is no passage in the New Testament that announces the withdrawal of healing or miraculous gifts. The standard cessationist text — 1 Corinthians 13:10, 'when completeness comes, the partial will disappear' — is read by many serious scholars as referring to the return of Christ, not the closing of the canon. No text in Scripture says: 'These signs were for the apostolic age only.'

Second, it is contradicted by church history. Healing and miraculous gifts did not disappear at the end of the first century. They are documented throughout church history — in the writings of the early fathers, in the Celtic church, in the medieval period, and with increasing frequency from the seventeenth century onwards. The claim that miracles ceased is simply not historically accurate.

> *"These signs will follow those who believe: In my name they will cast out demons; they will speak with new tongues… they will lay hands on the sick, and they will recover."* — **Mark 16:17-18**

Praying for Healing with Faithfulness and Humility

Believing in Jesus the healer does not mean adopting a naive or formulaic approach to prayer. Those of us who have prayed faithfully for healing and seen it received joyfully must also be honest about times when healing has not come in the way we hoped, or in the timing we prayed for. This is not a comfortable place, but it is an honest one.

Here is what we can say with confidence. When we pray for the sick, we are being obedient to the explicit command of Jesus. When we anoint the sick with oil and pray, we are following the instructions of the apostle James (James 5:14). Whether or not healing is immediate, the person being prayed for receives something real: the love of God mediated through the hands and prayers of God's people. That is never nothing.

We should also remember that Jesus himself sometimes prayed for a person more than once. There is a beautiful account in Mark 8 of a blind man who, after the first prayer, sees people but describes them as 'walking like trees.' Jesus prays again, and the man's sight is fully restored. If the Son of God prayed more than once for someone's healing, we need not feel that persistence in prayer is a sign of unbelief. It may be the most faithful thing we can do.

What we must never do is make the sick person feel responsible for their lack of healing. We are called to pray, to believe, and to leave the outcomes with a God who loves the person we are praying for far more than we do.

An Act of Obedience

Ultimately, praying for the sick is not primarily a strategy or a technique. It is an act of obedience.

> *"Heal the sick, raise the dead, cleanse those who have leprosy, drive out demons. Freely you have received; freely give."* — **Matthew 10:8**

Jesus gave this instruction not only to the Twelve but, in Luke 10, to the seventy-two — a much wider group of ordinary followers. The implication is clear: healing prayer is not the preserve of spiritual superstars or professionally ordained ministers. It is the ordinary vocation of every follower of Jesus. We freely received a Gospel that included miraculous demonstration of God's power and love. We are called, just as freely, to give it away.

CHAPTER THREE

Christ the Baptiser

Power for the Journey

A Promise from the Wilderness

Long before Jesus began His public ministry, a strange and compelling figure appeared in the wilderness of Judea. He wore camel's hair and ate locusts and wild honey. He baptised people in the Jordan River in an act of public repentance. And he pointed, with absolute consistency, beyond himself to one who was coming after him.

> *"I baptise you with water for repentance. But after me comes one who is more powerful than I, whose sandals I am not worthy to carry. He will baptise you with the Holy Spirit and fire."* — **Matthew 3:11**

I baptise with water. He will baptise with the Holy Spirit and fire. John drew a clear and deliberate contrast. His baptism was good and necessary — a public declaration of repentance, an alignment with the coming Kingdom. But it was, by John's own admission, a preparation. What was coming would be of an entirely different order.

The Promise the Disciples Were Told to Wait For

On the night before His crucifixion, Jesus made a remarkable promise to His frightened and confused disciples. He told them that He was going away — but that His going away was not abandonment. He would send them 'another advocate' (John 14:16), the Spirit of truth, who would be with them and in them. After the resurrection, this promise became even more specific.

> *"For John baptised with water, but in a few days you will be baptised with the Holy Spirit... you will receive power when the Holy Spirit comes on you; and you will be my witnesses in Jerusalem, and in*

> *all Judea and Samaria, and to the ends of the earth." —* **Acts 1:5, 8**

This is a striking command. These disciples had walked with Jesus for three years. They had heard His teaching, witnessed His miracles, and seen the risen Lord with their own eyes. And yet Jesus told them: you are not yet equipped for the task I am sending you to do. Wait for the power. What does this say about the importance of the Holy Spirit's empowering in the life of a believer? It says everything.

Two Aspects of One Spirit

The New Testament speaks about the work of the Holy Spirit in at least two complementary ways, and much of the confusion and division that has attended this topic in the modern church arises from failing to hold both together.

Paul, writing to the church in Corinth, speaks of the Spirit's work of incorporating us into the body of Christ: 'For we were all baptised by one Spirit so as to form one body' (1 Corinthians 12:13). This is the Spirit's initiating work. To be a Christian is to have been incorporated into Christ by the Spirit. But Luke — both in his Gospel and in the book of Acts — speaks repeatedly about a distinct empowering dimension of the Spirit's work. Luke records eleven references to this empowering baptism in the Spirit.

The two apostles — Paul and Luke — are not contradicting each other. They are describing different facets of the same diamond. The same Holy Spirit who unites us to Christ and gives us new birth is also the Spirit who empowers us for the mission Jesus has called us to. The question the New Testament invites us to ask is not 'which camp are you in?' but 'have you received all that Jesus promised to give you?'

The River and the Pool

In the forty-seventh chapter of Ezekiel, the prophet is given a remarkable vision. He sees water flowing from beneath the threshold of the Temple — first a trickle, then a stream, then a river that becomes too deep to cross, a river in which one must swim. Along the banks of this river, trees grow in abundance, bearing fruit in every season. The point of the vision is not that we arrive at ankle depth and stay there. The point is that there is always more — more of God, more of His life, more of His fruit-bearing power — available to those who are willing to wade deeper.

A pool requires you to do all the work. Your stroke provides the momentum, and the pool goes nowhere. But in a river, even floating takes you somewhere. The current does the work. The Christian life — the Spirit-filled, Spirit-empowered Christian life — is meant to be a river, not a pool.

> *"Let anyone who is thirsty come to me and drink. Whoever believes in me, as Scripture has said, rivers of living water will flow from within them."*
> **— John 7:37-38**

Come and Drink

The invitation of this chapter is simple and ancient. If you are thirsty — if something in you recognises that there is more to the Christian life than you have so far known — come. Come to Jesus. Not to a doctrine. Not to an experience. To Him.

He is still the Baptiser. He still immerses His people in the Holy Spirit and in fire. He still equips ordinary, unimpressive followers to do things that could not be done in their own strength. The book of Acts is not a historical curiosity. It is a description of normal Christian community when the Spirit is given His proper place. God does not want us to stagnate. The question is whether we are willing to let go of the side of the pool.

CHAPTER FOUR

Christ the Coming King

Living with an Eternal Horizon

The Most Neglected Element

Of the four dimensions of the Gospel we have explored in this book, this is perhaps the one that has fallen into the deepest silence in the contemporary church. Salvation is preached. Healing is, in many circles, tentatively embraced. The Holy Spirit's empowering is experiencing something of a renewal across denominations. But the return of Christ — the urgent, glorious, world-altering expectation that the King is coming — has largely been evacuated from the regular preaching of the Western church.

The reasons for this are understandable, if not entirely defensible. The topic has attracted its share of sensationalism: date-setters whose predictions have repeatedly embarrassed the church, elaborate prophetic charts that have intimidated ordinary believers, and popular fiction that has sold millions of copies while arguably distorting the biblical picture. But silence on the return of Christ is not caution. It is a form of disobedience to the plain teaching of Scripture, and a deprivation of the hope that the New Testament insists is central to Christian living.

The Promise

> *"Let not your hearts be troubled. Believe in God; believe also in me. In my Father's house are many rooms. If it were not so, would I have told you that I go to prepare a place for you? And if I go and prepare a place for you, I will come again and will take you to myself, that where I am you may be also."* **— John 14:1-3**

I will come again. These words were spoken directly, without qualification, to the people who loved Jesus most — the people who were about to watch Him be arrested, tried, and executed. In the darkest moment of their lives, He gave them an anchor: this is not the end. I am going, but I am coming back. The rest of the New Testament returns to this theme with remarkable consistency. Paul writes about it in his letters to the Thessalonians with the explicit purpose of comfort and encouragement. Peter addresses it in his second letter with the instruction to live in readiness and holiness. John ends the entire Bible with the prayer Maranatha — 'Come, Lord Jesus.'

The Jewish Wedding and the Returning Bridegroom

To understand the full emotional and theological weight of Jesus' promise in John 14, it helps enormously to understand the context in which His first hearers would have received it. In first-century Jewish culture, the prospective bridegroom would travel from his father's house to the house of the bride, negotiate the marriage covenant, and pay the agreed price. Then the bridegroom returned to his father's house — not to abandon the bride, but to prepare a place for her there.

The bride, meanwhile, did not know exactly when her bridegroom would return. She knew he was coming, and she prepared herself. When Jesus told His disciples, 'I go to prepare a place for you, and I will come again,' every Jewish person in that room would have heard a bridegroom making his vow. The imagery was unmistakable, the promise profound. This is why the New Testament describes the final culmination of all things as 'the marriage supper of the Lamb' (Revelation 19:9). History is not a random succession of events. It is a love story, moving toward a wedding.

What We Know and What We Don't

The details of how and when Christ's return will unfold are genuinely complex, and sincere, biblically serious Christians have reached different conclusions about the sequence of events, the nature of the millennial reign, and the relationship between the church and the tribulation period described in apocalyptic Scripture. Here is a working principle that has served well: the more dogmatic a person is about the precise mechanics of end-times chronology, the more likely they are to be wrong about some of it. He wants us to be ready, not to be timeline-managers.

What we do know, and what we can say without qualification: Jesus is really returning. Not metaphorically. Not spiritually. Bodily, visibly, with a shout and the sound of a trumpet — the same Jesus who ascended bodily from the Mount of Olives, whose return was announced to the watching disciples by two angels: 'This same Jesus... will come back in the same way you have seen him go into heaven' (Acts 1:11).

Living in the Light of His Coming

If Jesus is truly coming back — if the King is genuinely on His way — how does that change the way I live today? The Apostle Peter asks exactly this question in his second letter. After describing the cosmic dimensions of Christ's return, he pauses and asks: 'Since all these things are thus to be dissolved, what sort of people ought you to be in lives of holiness and godliness, waiting for and hastening the coming of the day of God?' (2 Peter 3:11–12).

The answer the New Testament returns, again and again, is threefold. We are to live with hope — the robust, certain expectation of people who know the end of the story. We are to live with urgency — because the people around us have not yet heard the Gospel, and the time is short. And we are to live with readiness — as the wise bridesmaids in Jesus' parable, who kept their lamps trimmed and their oil filled, prepared for the arrival that would come when least expected.

> *"And so we will be with the Lord forever. Therefore encourage one another with these words."* — **1 Thessalonians 4:17-18**

The return of Christ is not a source of fear for those who know Him. It is the ultimate encouragement. Every sorrow will be healed. Every injustice will be addressed. Every tear will be wiped away. The One who loves us is coming — and His coming changes everything.

CHAPTER FIVE

The Kingdom Now and Not Yet

Understanding What Jesus Actually Came to Build

The Remark That Changes Everything

The New Testament scholar and theologian Gordon Fee once made a remark that is simple enough to quote in a sentence but profound enough to spend a lifetime unpacking. He said: you cannot know anything about Jesus if you miss the Kingdom of God.

The Kingdom of God is not a peripheral theme in the Gospels. It is the central organising concept of everything Jesus taught and everything He did. Matthew's Gospel records Jesus using the phrase 'the Kingdom of heaven' more than thirty times. Mark opens his account of Jesus' ministry with a single, programmatic declaration: 'The time has come. The Kingdom of God has come near. Repent and believe the good news' (Mark 1:15). The Kingdom is the news.

Into the World Jesus Entered

To understand why the announcement of the Kingdom was such explosive news, we need to feel the weight of the world Jesus stepped into. The Jewish people of the first century were living under Roman occupation, waiting with burning expectation. The prophets had spoken of a coming King — a Messiah, from the line of David — who would deliver them from their enemies, restore the glory of Israel, and establish a Kingdom that would never end. When Jesus arrived in Galilee preaching that the Kingdom of God was at hand, it detonated like a signal flare in that tinderbox of expectation.

> *"Once, on being asked by the Pharisees when the kingdom of God would come, Jesus replied: The coming of the kingdom of God is not something that can be observed, nor will people say, 'Here it*

> *is,' or 'There it is,' because the kingdom of God is in your midst."* — **Luke 17:20-21**

The Messiah They Needed, Not the One They Expected

There is a painful irony woven through the Gospel accounts. The people who had studied the Scriptures most carefully were the people most likely to miss what God was actually doing when He arrived. Their expectations — shaped by centuries of suffering, entirely understandable, deeply sincere — had become a lens that filtered out the very thing they were looking for.

They expected a conquering king. They got a servant who washed feet. They expected an army. They got a band of fishermen and tax collectors. They expected the overthrow of Rome. They got a Kingdom that would overthrow something far more powerful than any empire: sin, death, and the dominion of Satan over human souls.

Already — But Not Yet

Perhaps the most important concept in all of New Testament theology is what scholars call the 'already but not yet' of the Kingdom of God. The Kingdom has come. In the person of Jesus, the reign of God broke into human history in a new and decisive way. When Jesus cast out demons, the Kingdom came. When He healed the sick, the Kingdom came. When He died on the cross and rose from the grave, defeating sin and death at their root, the Kingdom came.

But the Kingdom has not yet fully arrived. There is still suffering. There is still injustice. There is still death. The powers of darkness have been decisively defeated but have not yet been finally removed. We live in the overlap — after the decisive victory of the cross, before the final consummation of all things at Christ's return.

There is a story that illustrates this beautifully. Towards the end of the Second World War, a Scottish chaplain and a professor named McDonald were both shot down behind enemy lines and held as prisoners of war in Germany. Some of the American prisoners had a makeshift radio. One day, they picked up a signal announcing that the German High Command had surrendered. Life in that camp was transformed overnight. Men who were still technically prisoners walked around singing, laughing, waving at the guards. Three days later the Germans fled, leaving the gates unlocked, and the prisoners walked out as free men.

But here is the thing: they had actually been free from the moment the news arrived. The victory was real before the liberation was visible. This is precisely where the people of God live in every generation. The victory has been won. Freedom is real and it is available now — 'If the Son sets you free, you will be free indeed' (John 8:36). And yet we await the full and final liberation, the day when the gates swing open permanently and the new creation is fully revealed.

What Happens When We Die?

Scripture teaches that upon death, our bodies go into the ground and our souls go to be with the Lord. The Apostle Paul describes being 'away from the body and at home with the Lord' (2 Corinthians 5:8). This is real, it is good, and it is immediate. But that is not the final destination. The New Testament is clear that at the return of Christ, our bodies and souls will be reunited. We will be raised in resurrection bodies — real, physical, glorified bodies — to live in a renewed creation, free from sin and all its effects.

The theologian N.T. Wright puts it with characteristic clarity: the final hope of the Christian is not to 'go to heaven when we die' and remain there forever. It is resurrection — the complete undoing of everything that the fall of humanity in the Garden of Eden unleashed upon God's good creation.

> *"God's dwelling place is now among the people, and he will dwell with them. They will be his people, and God himself will be with them and be*

their God. He will wipe every tear from their eyes. There will be no more death or mourning or crying or pain, for the old order of things has passed away." — **Revelation 21:3-4**

Living Between the Times

How, then, do we live faithfully in the overlap between the Kingdom that has come and the Kingdom that is coming? First, we live with honesty about the present — lament is not unbelief, it is faith that refuses to accept the present state of things as the final word. Second, we live with hope that is more than optimism — the confident expectation of people who know the end of the story. Third, we live with urgency — every day that Christ has not yet returned is another day in which someone who does not yet know Him can come home. And fourth, we live with readiness. The biblical call is simply this: live as though He might return today, and plan as though He might delay for another generation. Hold both. Stay ready.

The Kingdom Is the Point

Gordon Fee was right. You cannot know anything about Jesus if you miss the Kingdom of God — because the Kingdom of God is what Jesus came to announce, to inaugurate, and to one day bring to completion.

In the light of that story, salvation makes sense — because to be saved is to be transferred from one kingdom to another. Healing makes sense — because bodily wholeness is a sign of the Kingdom that is coming. The baptism of the Spirit makes sense — because the Spirit is the down payment of the life of the new age. And the return of Christ makes sense — because every story needs its ending, and this story ends with a King on His throne and His people home at last.

Maranatha. Even so, come, Lord Jesus.

Conclusion

Reclaiming the Complete Gospel

We began with a question: How big is your Gospel?

We have spent five chapters exploring the answer the New Testament offers: bigger than most of us have preached it, bigger than most of us have believed it, and bigger than most of us have lived it.

The Gospel of the Kingdom is not a diminished, domesticated message about personal morality and a ticket to heaven. It is the announcement of a Kingdom that is breaking into the present world — with saving power for the spiritually lost, healing power for the physically broken, empowering presence for the humanly inadequate, and transforming hope for the cosmically hopeless. It is the message that turned the ancient world upside down, and it is precisely the message that our world needs today.

The two eras of greatest Christian expansion in history — the first century and the twentieth and twenty-first centuries — shared a common theological grammar. They preached Christ as Saviour, and people were born again. They preached Christ as Healer, and people were made whole. They preached Christ as Baptiser, and communities were transformed by the power of the Spirit. They preached Christ as coming King, and people lived with a holy urgency that made the Kingdom visible to everyone around them.

What would it look like for our churches to recover this complete Gospel? It would mean preaching salvation without apology — with the same directness and confidence that Peter showed before the Sanhedrin. It would mean praying for the sick with genuine faith and compassionate persistence, whether or not healing is immediate. It would mean creating space for the Holy Spirit to move — to fill, to empower, to gift, to lead — rather than managing our services so carefully that He has nothing to do. It would mean teaching on the return of Christ with theological care and pastoral warmth, restoring to our congregations the hope that their Bridegroom is coming. And it would mean recovering the full vision of the Kingdom — not as an escape from the world but as the transformation of it.

None of this requires us to abandon intellectual rigour, to leave our theological convictions at the door, or to pretend that these are simple and uncontested topics. It requires us to be like the scribe in Jesus' parable who 'brings out of his storeroom new treasures as well as old' (Matthew 13:52) — people who hold the ancient truths with fresh hands, who preach the old Gospel as though it is the best news in the world, because it is.

Jesus is the Saviour. He is the Healer. He is the Baptiser. He is the coming King. And His Kingdom — already present, not yet fully revealed — is the greatest story ever told.

That is the Gospel of the Kingdom. Go — and preach it.

Study Guide

For Individual and Group Use

This study guide is designed to help you engage more deeply with each chapter, whether you are reading alone or working through the book with a small group. For each chapter you will find discussion questions, key scriptures to memorise, and personal reflection prompts.

Discussion questions are best explored in community — a small group, a Bible study, or even a conversation over coffee with a friend. The personal reflection prompts are designed to move the content from your head to your heart. You may wish to write your answers in a journal.

Introduction: How Big Is Your Gospel?

Discussion Questions

1. Before reading this book, how would you have answered the question 'What is the Gospel?' How might your answer change now?

2. The introduction distinguishes between Dogma, Doctrine, and Teaching. Can you think of a time when you treated a 'Teaching' as though it were 'Dogma'? What were the consequences?

3. Why do you think the complete fourfold Gospel is not more commonly preached today? What might be lost when parts of it are neglected?

Key Scriptures

Acts 4:12 *Salvation is found in no one else, for there is no other name under heaven given to mankind by which we must be saved.*

Personal Reflection

❖ In your own experience, which of the four dimensions of the Gospel have you most emphasised, and which have you most neglected? Why do you think that is?

❖ What would a church that holds together the complete Gospel look like in your community? What would need to change?

Chapter 1: Christ Our Saviour

Discussion Questions

1. Peter's statement in Acts 4:12 — 'there is no other name' — is one of the most exclusive claims in Scripture. How do you hold this truth with love and grace toward people of other faiths?

2. The chapter describes sin as 'missing the mark.' Does this description change how you think about sin compared to how you might have defined it before?

3. Salvation is described as a gift that must be received, not earned. Why is this distinction so important?

4. What is repentance, and why is it inseparable from salvation? Is repentance a one-time event, or is it ongoing in the Christian life?

Key Scriptures

John 14:6 *I am the way and the truth and the life. No one comes to the Father except through me.*

Ephesians 2:8-9 *For it is by grace you have been saved, through faith — and this is not from yourselves, it is the gift of God — not by works, so that no one can boast.*

Romans 10:9 *If you declare with your mouth, 'Jesus is Lord,' and believe in your heart that God raised him from the dead, you will be saved.*

Personal Reflection

❖ Can you describe in your own words the moment, or season, when you received Christ? If you have never done so, what is holding you back?

❖ Is there any area of your life in which you are still trying to earn God's approval rather than resting in the free gift of His grace?

❖ Think of someone in your life who does not yet know Christ. What step could you take this week to share the Gospel with them?

Chapter 2: Christ Our Healer

Discussion Questions

1. Acts 10:38 describes Jesus as one who 'went about doing good and healing all who were oppressed.' What does this tell us about the character of God? What does it mean for us today?

2. How would you respond to someone who told you that the age of miracles is over? What would you say, and what scriptures would you use?

3. The chapter discusses what to do when healing does not come immediately. How do we hold faith and honesty together when we pray for someone and they are not healed?

4. Have you ever prayed for someone's healing? What happened? What did you learn from the experience?

Key Scriptures

Hebrews 13:8 *Jesus Christ is the same yesterday and today and forever.*

James 5:14-15 *Is anyone among you sick? Let them call the elders of the church to pray over them and anoint them with oil in the name of the Lord.*

Matthew 10:8 *Heal the sick, raise the dead, cleanse those who have leprosy, drive out demons. Freely you have received; freely give.*

Personal Reflection

❖ Do you genuinely believe that Jesus heals today? If you have doubts, where do those doubts come from — Scripture, experience, or teaching you have received?

❖ Is there a physical, emotional, or relational need in your own life for which you have not yet asked God to bring healing?

❖ Who around you is sick or suffering? Could you offer to pray for them this week?

Chapter 3: Christ the Baptiser

Discussion Questions

1. John the Baptist promised one who would baptise with the Holy Spirit and fire. What do you think the 'fire' refers to? What evidence of that fire do you see in the early church?

2. Acts 1:8 connects the gift of the Spirit directly to power for witness. What does 'witness' look like in your own life and context?

3. The chapter describes the Ezekiel 47 vision of water rising from ankle to knee to waist to swimming depth. Where would you say you are in that progression? What would it look like to go deeper?

4. Jesus says 'let anyone who is thirsty come to me.' What do you think it means to be spiritually thirsty, and how do we cultivate that thirst?

Key Scriptures

Acts 1:8 *You will receive power when the Holy Spirit comes on you; and you will be my witnesses in Jerusalem, and in all Judea and Samaria, and to the ends of the earth.*

John 7:37-38 *Let anyone who is thirsty come to me and drink. Whoever believes in me, rivers of living water will flow from within them.*

Ephesians 5:18 *Do not get drunk on wine, which leads to debauchery. Instead, be filled with the Spirit.*

Personal Reflection

❖ How would you describe your experience of the Holy Spirit so far in your Christian life?

❖ Is there any part of your life where you are 'holding the side of the pool' — maintaining control — rather than surrendering to the current of the Spirit?

❖ Spend some time in prayer simply asking God to fill you afresh with His Spirit. Write down anything you sense or experience.

Chapter 4: Christ the Coming King

Discussion Questions

1. Why do you think the return of Christ is so rarely preached in many churches today? What is lost when this topic is neglected?

2. The Jewish wedding imagery in John 14 is used to explain Jesus' promise of His return. How does this picture change or deepen your understanding of His coming?

3. Peter asks: 'Since all these things are to be dissolved, what sort of people ought you to be?' How should the expectation of Christ's return practically shape the way we live?

4. How do we maintain theological humility about the details of end-times chronology while still preaching about Christ's return with conviction?

Key Scriptures

John 14:1-3 *Let not your hearts be troubled. Believe in God; believe also in me... I will come again and will take you to myself.*

1 Thessalonians 4:16-17 *For the Lord himself will descend from heaven... and so we will always be with the Lord.*

2 Peter 3:11 *Since everything will be destroyed in this way, what kind of people ought you to be? You ought to live holy and godly lives.*

Personal Reflection

❖ If Jesus returned today, what would you be glad about — and what would you wish you had done differently?

❖ Is the return of Christ a source of hope and anticipation for you, or does it produce anxiety? What shapes your response?

❖ Spend a few minutes writing a prayer expressing your response to the reality that Jesus is coming back.

Chapter 5: The Kingdom Now and Not Yet

Discussion Questions

1. Gordon Fee said you cannot know anything about Jesus if you miss the Kingdom of God. Do you agree? What do you think the 'Kingdom of God' actually means, in your own words?

2. The Jewish people of Jesus' day expected a political Messiah. In what ways do we today bring our own unexamined expectations to Jesus — expecting Him to be the kind of Saviour we want rather than the one we need?

3. The 'already but not yet' concept describes the Kingdom as genuinely present but not yet fully arrived. How does this framework help you make sense of why there is still suffering and injustice in a world where Jesus has already won?

4. The chapter argues that our final destination is not a disembodied heaven but a resurrected life in a renewed creation. Does this change how you think about the physical world, the body, or the value of your work here and now?

5. The POW illustration describes people who were free before they felt free. In what area of your life might you be living as a prisoner when the gates are already unlocked?

Key Scriptures

Mark 1:15 *The time has come. The Kingdom of God has come near. Repent and believe the good news.*

John 8:36 *If the Son sets you free, you will be free indeed.*

2 Peter 3:9 *The Lord is not slow in keeping his promise... he is patient with you, not wanting anyone to perish, but everyone to come to repentance.*

Revelation 21:3 *God's dwelling place is now among the people, and he will dwell with them. They will be his people, and God himself will be with them and be their God.*

Personal Reflection

❖ Where in your life do you find it hardest to live in the 'already' — to actually experience the freedom and Kingdom life that Christ has secured?

❖ Knowing that the final hope of Scripture is a renewed creation, does anything change about how you view your daily work, your relationships, or the way you care for the physical world around you?

❖ Write a short prayer in response to the 'already but not yet.' Be honest with God about where you feel the 'not yet' most acutely.

A Final Word

This study guide is a beginning, not an ending. The four dimensions of the Gospel explored in this book are not topics to be studied and set aside — they are realities to be lived, preached, and demonstrated in the world.

As you close this book, consider sharing it with someone. Discuss it with your small group, your family, your minister. Bring its questions to your church community. The Gospel of the Kingdom is not a private possession. It is good news — and good news is meant to be told.

The last prayer of the Bible is four words: Come, Lord Jesus. Amen.

Maranatha.

Salvation 4 All Ministries

Sharing the love of Jesus to all nations and all peoples

Salvation 4 All Ministries is an Australian charity registered with the ACNC. Nick Booth has been active in evangelism since his teenage years, and together with his wife Natasha has devoted over 25 years to church planting, youth leadership, and pastoral ministry across various contexts.

Nick partners with evangelists in crusades across Africa, Asia, and the Pacific, and is available for evangelism training and healing messages to local churches.

"The harvest is plentiful, but the workers are few.

Ask the Lord of the harvest to send out workers."

— Luke 10:2

Connect

www.salvation4all.com

s4aevangelism@gmail.com

Give to the Ministry

BSB: 063 882 | A/C: 1099 0851

salvation4all.com/donate